Pocket Prayers

June O'Leary

PublishAmerica
Baltimore

ISBN: 1-4241-1595-7
PUBLISHED BY PUBLISHAMERICA, LLLP
www.publishamerica.com
Baltimore

Printed in the United States of America

For my husband, my muse, my Justin

I'd like to acknowledge two of my teachers. Mrs. Hampson, who first predicted I'd be published, and M. LeDantec, who let me write my first poems on the chalkboard. Thank you!

Table of Contents

772.

I want to write things so profound
No one will forget them
Everyone will know them
They will finish arguments
The things I want to write

930.

Whisper down to me my angels, dead loved ones
Whisper what I need
Who to trust
Who to not
Walking with me
Shadows in my wake
Angels and dead loved ones
Answer to me
When I call your names in faith
Because faith is all you need
To make anything come true
Belief is the nature of truth
So protect me from the demons
Sweet angels and dead loved ones
And I'll remember to say thank-you

1,004.

She used to light up her cigarettes
Like it was some spiritual event
And maybe for her it was
She always said she had smoke in her soul
Her life a never-ending braid
Three strands of pain, love, and madness
Reflected in the triptych I made
And if the ones we love never really leave us
Then I suppose she isn't gone at all
She's here, inside of me
A little puff of smoke in my soul

120.

You find me when
I don't wanna be found
You push me away
Or you hold me down
But I'm still here
I'm still here
I'm still here

You burn me up
Then you blow me out
Get inside my head
You scream and shout
But I'm still here
I'm still here
I'm still here

1,044.

Sleeping
Stuck in amber
Dreaming of my life
And I know I'm stuck
Every day the same
No hope for change
It's not enough
Ask me
When I was happiest
The happiest moment of my life
It was raining outside
But I didn't care
I was spinning and laughing in the rain
No reason why
The happiest moment of my life
And I can see it
Kept in an amber glass
On a shelf in the house of black
But I can't get to it
Unless I stay there
Afraid of the unknown
But I do know
I'm already stuck
In the amber of this stagnant life
And if I'm to be stuck
I'd rather be stuck inside
The happiest moment of my life
A door opens in my dream
And I go through
Body and mind
Which is why you'll find me now
On a shelf in the house of black
Kept in an amber glass

Spinning and laughing in the rain inside
Stuck in amber
The happiest moment of my life

1,076. (Soldiering)

People asking why I never wear a smile
Why I'm so stone faced
Hide my eyes behind my shades
But can't you see the blood
Dripping from my hands
And can't you see the tears
Sliding down my face
Can't you see my tortured halo?
Could you forgive me?
I was just property
I was just the gun
I wasn't the one
Who gave the orders
I only pulled the trigger
Either them or me
Would you rather it had been me?
Came back to these states
Nothing like my father faced
At least they didn't spit
But I'm so lonely
I just can't relate
I'm in another state
Hear a shot, reach for my gun
Panic when it isn't there
Remember then where I really am
Just a car causing the scare
I don't wear a smile
But underneath my shirt
I wear my scars
A drunk shouting curses
I didn't take a bullet for you
But all you people with loving eyes
For you I took a few

But I can't talk to you
About three years of my life
And I'm afraid to meet your eyes
Hey Jesus
How's my halo doing?
My job was to protect
And I did with every bullet
But how do I tell them?
When they're asking about it?
Nothing like the movies
Blood dripping from my hands
Tears sliding down my face
You would forgive me
At least they don't spit
For loving eyes
I took the bullet
Hey Jesus
How's my halo?

109.

You know the sky is falling down
Slipping down my face like rain
Hit you on the head
You never hear me scream
And you know it's all gone black
Well darkness was her color
It's never coming back
There's nothing much I have to fear
But still you wish you had dared
It's getting cold inside of here
Though the world is night
A single crystal tear
And dreams clarify
The last has finally come
Why am I so terrified?
Though you know it's all come true
You had to have more
Before you took less
Things will always be the same
Something to think about

121.

Unborn snow fills the city
Unborn snow drifts over me
Unborn snow is hard to find
It's snow that hasn't quite become snow yet
And I myself cannot blame it
Who wants to take the final step?
Unborn snow make up your mind
See her dancing over there
As the light shines through the mist
Smell her sweet pixie essence
See the water in her hair?
Unborn snow brings out magic
Unborn snow calls the wild folk
Unborn snow can cure the sick
Unborn snow costs men their hearts
Unborn snow is unborn magic

226.

Up here alone in the sky
There is nothing to guide me
A goddess in my own life
I choose my own destiny
I go wherever my will directs
I soar towards the sun
I fly into the moon
High above everyone
There's only the sound of silence
Except for when I move
Then I can hear myself dig through the air
But no one can ever see the groove
I do not thirst
And I do not sleep
I'm naked as the birds
There are no secrets to keep
It's always warm
Night is the only shade
My wings are strong
I'm not afraid
It's almost overwhelming
Up here alone in the sky
Everything is open
Nothing here makes me cry
The wind and the clouds
Are the only things to feel
And there's nothing here to hold
I will stay until I heal
I know I cannot fall
There is no gravity
There is no hunger
There is only the meaning of free

228.

Words
Such sensual things
If I were to make a person from words
It would have to be a man
For men and women equally
Make feelings in me
Except sensuality
I have never been aroused by a woman
So it would have to be a man
My person of words
I adore men
Such beautiful creatures

229.

Hello
To whomever is reading these words
I'm writing this just for you
All right
I wrote this for others too
But whomever you are
The guy
Or the girl
Who just happened to read this
I want you to know
That I love you
Maybe I'm far away
Maybe we've never met
Maybe we never will
But having read this
You know me a little
Kiss these words
And wherever I am
I promise
I'll kiss you back

9.

I am in a box
A box with many locks
Who knows what lurks inside?
But luckily for me,
No one cares what it is I hide
So they all let it be
And nobody will ask
What lies beneath my mask

25.

Love is a shoulder to cry upon
Love is a feeling warm as the dawn
Love is an embrace tight and strong as lead
Love is gentle kisses at the back of your head
And if you love your love with all of your heart
Then love is an ocean no ship can ever chart

74.

You haven't been around
I wrote to you
Was it frightening?
I didn't mean to tell
You make me wonder
So many things
It frightens me
Would you set me right?
I didn't mean to tell
We don't have to change now
Just keep going
Let our friendship stay?
I didn't mean to tell
Are we through
'Cause of what I told you?
Stay won't you please
And my secret keep?
I didn't mean to tell
That I love you

87.

I went to sleep with you in my head
And awoke to find you in my bed
How gently
How softly
How sweetly
You kissed me
And how the tears fell and my heart broke
When the dream ended and I awoke

423.

You can't stop me
From laughing and singing out loud to myself
You can't stop me
From enjoying this thing called life
You can't stop me
I don't care if you think I'm crazy
You can't stop me

260.

I'm inside you now
You may forget my face for a time
I won't cross your mind for years
But eventually
You will remember me
The way I stretch my neck
The movements of my eyes
How I'd sing along with the radio
And sit with my legs swinging
I'm inside you now
The instant you met me
I became
A part of you
The inflections in my voice
When I spoke to you
The exact sound of my laugh
How I'd just hang around
And watch you
How you wondered
What I was doing
I'm inside you now
Ever since you looked at me
I've been within your memory
How I looked into you
Without fear
But with acceptance
Like I was a part of you
I'm inside you now

410.

I couldn't close my eyes
Couldn't turn my head
When Truth so fiercely
Glared up at me
Did you know they were lies
The things that they said
When we were children
No more Virtue
The right thing to do
Isn't always true
No more Virtue
No more
There are no ideal worlds
So they don't apply
Only Truth exists
Still we dismiss
The facts as they're unfurled
And then we ask why
Our system won't work
No more Virtue
The right thing to do
Isn't always true
No more Virtue
No more

435.

They were strange
Subtle angels
Led to you
Enslaved every wish
Every dream
All hopes
With you
Temptation
I resisted
But still
I am corrupted
I can never have you
I will forever want you
Because I was blind
I did not see their horns
Did not know
They'd fallen
I only knew
They were strange
Subtle angels

501.

Persephone
She wears a locket
'Round her neck
It is round and circular
Symbol of eternity
And it is golden
The color of value
It hangs on a velvet cord
Tied in a knot
Forever binding
Not like a clasp
That can be undone
Inscribed on the cover is a heart
Symbol of love
And the picture inside is of a skull
Her beloved husband Death

222.

Would you gather up my feathers
As they fall from my wings
Would you sew them back together
So I can fly again
Because I can't stay here for long
My need for the sky is too strong
It's a sad life for a pixie
It's a hard life for an angel
And it's a sad hard life for me
Without wings to fly
Would you sew these wings to my skin
My blood's as red as yours
After all I'm only human
Now I can fly once more
And if I crash and burn and die
I'll thank God for letting me fly
It's a sad life for a pixie
It's a hard life for an angel
And it's a sad hard life for me
Without wings to fly on

148.

Loving you is a
Razor-winged butterfly
Cutting through my heart

133.

Still we see
What we don't want
Everywhere
The mountains look gaunt
I could watch you all day
I could touch you all night
I could repeat things you say
But I could mean it
People aren't your puppets my dear
That's not why they come
And not why I'm here
You watch far apart
As you pierce my heart
Glance as my blood pours out
See the moments fly by
Hear every lie
Love and Trust
The keys to eternal bliss
I'll never stop being in love
Though I stopped trusting
And I forgave you
But not myself

225.

Walking down the street
It's never people that you meet
It's fans meeting you
Asking for a picture or two
When you smile at them
Do their eyes widen?
People think they know who you are
How does it feel to be a star?

234.

Some people write diaries
Recording dates, events, facts
Things that are over and done with
I write poetry
Recording dreams, emotions, thoughts
Things that never end

247.

I am woman
See my curves
My hairless flesh
And my red lipstick
Smell my perfume
Feel my smoothness
I adorn myself
In velvet
And in lace
Because I am beautiful
I am woman
See my curves

502.

Friends and family are gathered
A preacher speaks
A woman should always wear white
A man should always be in suit and tie
And flowers yes
There must always be flowers
At a wedding
Or a funeral
Same thing
Dearly departed
Dearly beloved
We are gathered here
'Til death do us part
'Til death do us reunite
End of my life
Beginning of our life
End of mortality
Beginning of immortality

509.

Those with suicidal tendencies remember:
The living *can* love
The dead can only rot

515.

Going to see my newborn niece
When "Todd's dead" Grandpa says
"Take a minute then see the baby"
Beautiful baby, beautiful Todd
Tall, tan, never could grow a mustache
Small, pink, dark hair like her momma
Please God please, let it be mistaken identity
We were three's and four's playing at Grandma's
I was the princess, Todd the hero
I was five, asked Momma
"Can I marry Todd?"
"Oh honey, he's your cousin"
Visited not too long ago
He twisted my arm
He "Say I'm the master"
Me "No—OW!"
But never really hurt anyone
Swerved not to hit an animal and FLIP!
Mow the critters down next time
Scared, he must have been
Grandpa speaks during service, chokes
My nephew three "Where's Todd?"
Choked to say "Heaven"
We all die sometime
Why this time?
Why our Todd?
He was coming here for school
Supposed to be welcoming him
Not saying goodbye
But humans make mistakes
And God was human
To the statue of Christ "I forgive you"
How horrid to outlive your child

To outlive your grandchild
Grandpa asked "When will you make me a great-grandfather?"
"Todd will probably beat me to it"
He said "I don't think so"
Now we know so
Wednesday I was oldest of fifteen grandkids
Thursday sixteen
Friday fifteen
Wednesday's child full of woe
Our family is
Big Italian family
Always kiss and hug
Closed casket
Can't even see
Can't kiss him goodbye

532.

My love I gave you my love
You were to have returned my love with a kiss
Instead you returned my love with a "no thanks"
My love has returned my love
It seems my love is not enough for my love
But my love is still my love

503.

In a house of poets
Madness reigns
Words have logarithmic meanings
Moods are feigned
Or else deeply sincere
One never knows
In a house of poets

1,096.

Sitting next to you
Always such a lovely view
Hazel eyes
And shaggy hair
The nose I want to bite
I feel I am at peace
And all my sorrows released
Birds flying away
They'll come back some day
That's life
I accept that
But I'm always relieved
When I reach out to
And find you

49.

I awoke and saw Death racing through the sky
And as I stared into his cold empty eye,
I knew that it were my blood he'd come to thirst,
When God appeared beside me and said, "Take Me first."

1,115.

The sky couldn't hold me
It said good luck baby
And as I fall
I'll sing you away
As I'm falling
I'll sing you awake
Make me no promises
I'll tell you no lies
Give me your oceans
I'll give you my skies
You know this girl's a handful
And I'll tell you why
Momma's Italian and Dad is Irish
You sure you can handle this girl?
I'll sing you your praises
While you sing your flaws
I'm your confessor
With the loudest applause
No one will ever be true
No one will ever know truth
Like I do
Like I know you
My affection
My reflection
Your affection
Your reflection
Mirror, mirror, mirror
I'll sing you to pieces
Your own apocalypse
At innocent hands
Just like you wanted it
Tear you apart
Husk your shell

Shred your mask
'Til there's no more hiding
Finally at last
And you're new
And you're raw
Like a new life
Filled with new light
That I bring to my cheek
Love forever and keep
I'll sing you a song of your troublesome past
I'll sing you your future once the die has been cast
You wanted a sign
So I'm flashing neon
So come on
Come on
I'll sing you all day
Like a bird in a cage
The sky couldn't hold me
It said see you baby
Give me your oceans
I'll give you my skies
Make me no promises
I'll tell you no lies
As I fall
Lose my wings
As I fall
No more wings
Only song

583.

There are many creatures here beneath the sea
Slowly nibbling away at me
Swimming in my hair, feasting on my eyes
Chewing on lips that never told lies
They shall get to my brain eventually
And eat my every memory
The sea has softened my skin
You'd like me now, I am so thin
My heart still loves you unconditionally
And when the fish try to take it from me
They'll weep because then they'll all love you
Until the ocean rises and swallows you too
And your bones rest with mine for all eternity
Together forever, just you and me
Although I admit, not how I wanted it to be

607.

There are seven things which everyone should try at least once:
Having ice cream for breakfast
Sticking your head out the window of a speeding car
Reading *Ulysses*
A bubble bath
Kissing
Walking barefoot on fresh snow
And karaoke!

609.

The four hardest things to fully accept are:
Bad things happen to good people
You have to work to succeed
Love doesn't conquer all
And God is not to blame

625.

Virtue need not be cold
Vice need not be perverse
Love in trust
Love in lust
Together in devotion
There's no end to their motion

648.

When you died
I didn't believe it was you
I wanted to open the coffin
I wanted to see
I wanted to know
But they wouldn't let me
Then I dreamt
I dug you up
And opened your coffin
And you were a mess
But I could see
That it was you
So I kissed you goodbye
And laid you back to rest
Now though I still cry
I find myself laughing too
It's you
I can stop worrying now
It's you

688.

You can't see me as I am
Only what you perceive
If you are perceiving me
You are not seeing me
If you're not seeing me
I may as well go masked
You'll perceive the mask
For my true face
And not as a fake
So I can manipulate you
Through what you perceive
But we all love to deceive
You can't see me
You can't see me as I am
Only what you perceive

875.

The little children almost grown
Surging under the weight of the band
I wander past and into a side room
And don't you think it's time now?
Looking down the table and there you are
Winking over champagne glasses
You hold me and I hear your pulse race
And don't you think it's time now?
The steel castles reign far above
But they don't rule those of us below
'Cause the music can make them tumble down
And don't you think it's time now?
The city thrives beneath the stars
Tired we lean into one another
We're in the post-show limbo babydoll
And don't you think it's time now?

608.

You thought you were so much better than me
But I got news for you
You were wrong
You know why?
Because the video store at the corner just got the latest
independent British film
And I rented it first!
So when you go to the video store at the corner and try to rent the
latest independent
British film
And find they're all out
I want you to know that I'll be watching the latest independent
British film and eating
popcorn
I know you'll be upset
I know you won't be able to sleep because you won't stop
thinking about me and the
latest independent British film
You'll get up at two in the morning to use the potty because you
can't sleep
Then you'll use the last squares of toilet paper off the roll and
won't replace it
So when you get up in the morning and go to use the potty you'll
have to look under the
sink
Then you'll realize you're all out!
In which case I want you to know that not only did I get to see the
latest independent
British film and you didn't
But I bought a whole new pack of toilet paper the day before
I want you to think about that all day when you're at work
So that you can't concentrate
Sometimes I'll be in my office at work and I can't concentrate
either

That's when I put on a CD and hum along to lovely Irish music
It helps me refocus you know?
Wait a second…
You don't know do you?!
You don't have a CD player at your work
In fact you're still flipping burgers at the drive-thru!
Well I want you to know that I have my own office with a CD
player and two windows!
Mmm-hmh
Now I bet you're wondering why I'm enjoying this
Rest assured I *am* enjoying this
But it's not because you were popular in high school and I wasn't
Not because your dad bought you a car when you turned sixteen
and I had to ride the bus
Not because you wouldn't let me into your group
Not even because you stole my boyfriend and went to the prom
with him while I stayed
home and cried
I'm doing this because you went out of your way to make my life
shit and now I get to
return the favor
By the way…
My new boyfriend brought me some gifts from Louisiana
Isn't he sweet?
Of course you haven't had a decent boyfriend since you stole
mine
But all I want you to know is that not only did I get to see the
latest independent British
film
And not only do I have a wonderful boyfriend who spoils me,
my own office with two
windows, a CD player, and *lots* of toilet paper
Mmm-hmh
But now I also have a voodoo doll with your name on it
Have a nice day!

723.

You keep winking
You keep winking like we share
Some deep secret
You keep looking
You looking at me like
I'm your whole world
Are you sure?
You keep acting
You keep acting so charming
It's suspicious
You keep saying
You keep saying you're in love
But is it true?
Are you sure?
You keep smiling
You keep smiling sexily
But you know I...
I'm not like other girls
If you want me
You have to do more than
Wink
Look
Act
Say
Or smile
You have to be
I mean you have to BE
Mine
My one and only
Forsaking all others
Are you ready?
Are you ready for me now?
Do you want me?
Are you sure?

710.

There was a china doll
And it was happy sitting on the shelf
Then a child picked it up and danced
Then put it back on the shelf
And the china doll thought,
"That was fun"
Then another child picked it up and danced
And put it back
And the china doll thought,
"I can hardly wait to dance again"
Then a third child came along
And picked it up and danced
And this one danced so long
The china doll thought,
"This will last forever"
And just when the china lips
Almost broke into a china smile
The china doll was tossed back on the shelf
And it waited a long time
But no more children wanted to dance
And china tears could have broken the china face
Then the china doll climbed down from the shelf
And started to dance
All alone by itself

748.

I can't keep it up
All this mystery
It just isn't me
It gets harder to pretend
And I don't think that I can
Not be who I really am
But when the mask falls
The audience gasps
And nobody claps
Can't we just accept ourselves
Or are we all forced to be
Reflections of what we see
Let's break our mirrors
Step out of the glass
Go against the mass
Because there's only so long
We have to show the outside
What we really have inside

915.

With pain and prayer
You are still there
Whenever I turn my head
But you must swear
To go elsewhere
And let me sleep when I'm dead

916.

Momma said
And Daddy swore
You just can't tell anymore
So keep an Easter reed
And a loaded gun
On hand when you answer the door

922.

Standing in the light
Looking out
To the dark
Hearing whispers
Beyond the bright songs
Pretty girls
And lovely boys
Hiding inside themselves
Night protecting day
For the jaded world
Cares for blue skies
As much as true hearts
And yearning minds
Darlings
Sweet darlings
Stay inside the light
And I know
You will blind them
The doubters

630.

I thank my heavenly father
For the musky scent of men
For the deepness of their voices
And the stubble on their chin
For the muscles and the strong arms
That give loving protection
For the demands of their kisses
And the moans of their passion
I thank my heavenly father
For the man I love, Amen

639.

My eyes play tricks
Trick trick
Trip trip
Fall down
I didn't see
The ground
My eyes were playing
Tricks
Someone shine
So bright I'm blind
No more
To see
Such beauty
No more
To be
Tricked
Am I really here?
And are you really there?
My eyes keep playing
Tricks
The fuzzy edge
Of your vision
Is where I am
Is where I'll be
Not always remembered
But still
A good memory
When your eyes
Play tricks on me

685.

Drop down
Through the fabric
Of this reality
Let me hold you
As you sobbing
Confide it all in me
Hiding
In plain sight
It's all so easy
Just let
Me guard you
And you will soon see
Stronger than strong
Softer than soft
What you want it to be
Drop down
Through the fabric
Of this poorly made reality
Let me hold you close to my heart
As you sobbing
Confide it all in me
We'll gather it all up
And make it into
What you want it to be
And afterwards
If you still want comfort
All you do is call me

692.

Whisper me awake
Alert all my nerves
Call the sun to rise
Open up my eyes
Bring me gentle noise
I'll give you kisses
Passion
Hunger
Love and pain
Now you lie contained
Smiling
Sighing
Warm and safe
Now kiss my eyes closed
Bring me sweet quiet
Call the sun to set
Deaden all my nerves
Whisper me asleep

1,014.

As you slid down into my dreams
I was talking to you
About music, books, and things
You smiled so softly
I couldn't believe it was me you were smiling at
We drove into the desert
The darkness had me a little scared
But you said it would be okay
You had driven this way before
And I tried reciting poetry
But I'd forgotten all the words
The day lit up
Sun rose like a slow jack-in-the-box
It was beautiful the way your face looked
As you watched it
Wish I'd had a camera
We chatted along
Never ran out of things to say or hear
We listened hard
And I'd never spoken so long in my life
But you didn't mind
Just laughed at my jokes and passed the water
And I had never heard
Such stories as you told
But then you said, "We're almost there"
The mountains I call home stretched before us
I knew the truck would have to stop and let me out
But I wasn't sure
You'd remember to call me sometime
So I just looked at you
And held onto your smile

1,032.

In a room of sweet scent candles
There's not enough light
To keep back the monsters
Chewing their way
Through the walls
It's one a.m.
And time again
To beg for sleep
Beg your release
And you know us Catholics
Saints for everything
Seven holy sleepers
From a Russian fairy tale
To give me comfort

1,033.

You didn't say if you'd come back
Nothing hurts as not knowing
Afraid to speak
Afraid to breathe
Because of your powder keg
I climb down
Down in the basement
The racing cars pass me by
And I walked with the angels
Rapt attention paid to pain
Holding on to love's hand
And laughed at the madness
Walking along the lunatic road
Watch your feet for broken glass
As you spy the bread crumbs left
To lead you deeper in
Where darkness needs no light
To define itself complete
And you call go no farther
But I can't fight the current
All the fight's gone from me
No more pain or even madness
Just the absence of love left

831.

I dream
I dream of a half-dozen goddesses
All with my face
Living in a house
Its exterior painted black
Even the windows
Like an ink blot
In the historical downtown area
The neighbors don't come by
But the children do
The goths and punks and hippies
The quiet mousy bookish ones
And some adults who haven't lost it:
That frail tattered lace of innocence
With its worrying threads of insecurity
Poetica and Madness
Love and Silence
And the ever-present twins:
Vice and Virtue
Entertain their guests
With stories and pictures
Songs and ideas
Until the guests feel inspired enough to leave
To pursue their rekindled imaginings
In one form or another of creativity
Such is the way of artists:
To abandon their muses
But I somehow doubt these six mind
They seem to enjoy their time alone
Together in the blackened house
When they can open treasures so bright
No mortal eyes could see
So bright

The paint on the windows
Is necessary
I dream of them
I dream

805.

Mother distributed the host
And my father carpeted
Our Father's house
I have too many dead relatives
Visiting me
For death to truly frighten me
It's the things I have planned
That I haven't finished yet
That worry me
And now I know
I usually get what I pray for
Eventually

756.

You're forever like an angel
Mourning for the fallen leaves of autumn
Gathering tears within your eyes
As the yellow leaves surround your feet
You do not cry
For it will not bring life back
To what is dead
Instead you turn from the sky
With bowed head
And whisper through your solicitude
Solace to the trees
That they will be green again

911.

What do you want?
For what would you fight?
Kisses to the blackbirds...
Looking from above
Your eyes so innocent, awed
As if never before
They believed in God
Kisses to the blackbirds...
They've waited so long...
When you go home
Do you claim nothing happened?
Hey sleepy eyes
Why such a need to pretend?
Kisses to the blackbirds...
They've waited so long...
So long...
So long...
Tied down inside
Locked away in the closet
Empty chested
My heart deep in your pocket
Kisses to the blackbirds...
They've waited so long...
They've waited so long to kill you...
So long...
So long...

927.

Mother cradles her forgotten child
Forgotten lest remembered
We never hear your sighs anymore
We never see the skies anymore
Forgotten on purpose
Those reckless emotions
Pain and hope
Left stored away
Safely where they cannot hurt
'Cause tears get you nothing
Sorrow and grief
Just getting in the way
People aren't nice to nice persons
So happy faces worthless too
Locked up tight
Out of sight
Children in the streets
In the park
You never hear their cries
You only see their eyes
'Cause they know much better than we did
They know what they get and what with
Mother forgive them
Mother forgive me, and us
We never meant to forget
We just forgot on purpose

929.

Pocket prayers
Whispered any everywhere
Private lines straight to You
Testing, testing
One two and three
I can't find what it means
Hello, is the Almighty there?
The greyhounds protect me
Turbo and Pooh-Bear
Back from the dead
To play more games of fetch
I feel my pocket
For another prayer
As certainty grips me
I'll never see him again
Pocket prayers
Listening to them preach
Pocket prayers
Helping me to bear
What shouldn't have been there
The coffin standing there
Testing, testing
One two and three
I'm waiting for the meaning
I've been on hold for so long
Hello, may I have the Almighty?
Another pocket prayer
To see you through the night
To bring you safely where
Our life goes on as one
I told the spirits I love you
That I'd destroy if they'd harm you
A car crumpled on its side

My loved one dead inside
Reach for a pocket prayer
Years passed and it's still there
The fear and the anger
Of what should not have been
Knowing it may happen again
Testing, testing
One two and three
I need to know the meaning
Can't wait until I'm dead
Can I leave the Almighty a message?
I've got my pocket prayers
I've got my dead dogs
I've got my memories
Of the cousin You didn't save
The lover You might have failed too
Call me with the answers
'Cause I'm trying to forgive You
And thank You for my pocket prayers
Couldn't do without my pocket prayers

1,080.

There's no future in dance
Art is dying
In all its aspects
The thing is, they polluted it
By trying to make a buck off it
One day we'll all wake up
And go to work in suits
It's not a bad thing
It's evolution
But we can't evolve anymore
I mean physically
Mentally we could
If we used our imaginations
We could save ourselves then
But the alchemists discredited themselves
With their poison mercury fumes
So their genius insights are gone
And science is the new religion
That sounds like a cute catch phrase
Don't it?
But it's true
They even have organized churches
So the arts are dying
And our potential fades
One day God will wipe us out and start again
He's done it before
Quite a few times
Maybe next time it'll be perfect
And they'll be meek
The ones who inherit the Earth
But we'll still be here
All of us as ghosts
We'll entertain them

Be their television
Tell them our stories
Of what we were
What we did
And they won't understand
But they'll smile like angels
The Perfect Ones

1,086.

I'm not here to be seen
I'm not here to be heard
Not even supposed to speak
I'm only here to observe
All the name droppers 'round here
They're like a new species
Homo sapien vicarious
Like a psychic disease
I'm not saying I'm better
Than anybody else
Just when I look in the mirror
I recognize myself
This is the story of the world
Wanting everything
Except what's already yours
My advice
Don't sell yourself short

1,064.

He claims I'm the moon
In his nighttime sky
Smiling on the world
In its daytime hours
During his long sleep
Claims I make him glow
Me his light and warmth
Me his energy
And I love him so
His strength too my own
He says it better
God gave me talent
Only to write it
So I write my love
If I were the moon
He would be the sky
Without him I'd fall
But he surrounds me
Ever embracing
Holding me secure

652.

I always thought that was stupid
Marrying someone because you think you can change them
If you marry someone
It should be because you love them
And if you love someone
It should be because of who they are
Not who you think they could become

663.

I admire people
Who are more like candles than neon lights
Candle flames shine
While neons only glow
All candles can be pleasantly scented
No neons can stop from buzzing obnoxiously
Flames give warmth
And cast shadows
Neon does neither
And a candle only stops
When there is nothing left of itself
Whereas an elaborate elegant neon
Always leaves a heap of useless glass
That's also why I like candles

682.

Baby please tell me
Why you act this way
Too old to be colicky
And if you want to cry
I'll sing you sweet lullaby
Goodbye my darling
Goodbye my love
Goodbye my sorrow
Goodbye you were all the above
Baby is still crying
Inside of my mind
Tell my mind
Just to never mind
Baby's still crying
When all I did was as asked
I said goodbye to Baby
Said goodbye to it all
Look into the mirror
Kiss my lips goodnight
Baby's at last quiet

1,089.

Baby blue angel
He fell from the sky
Fell from so high
He ought to have died
But didn't even cry
Baby blue angel
Baby blue angel

Sad little witch
Born in a ditch
Escaped from her room
On a magical broom
Fell outta the sky
Fell pretty far
Hit pretty hard
But she didn't cry
Sad little witch
Sad little witch

Where are your tears?
What is it you fear
So much you can't cry?
I'll sing you goodbye
With my strange lullaby
But please don't cry
Sing you goodbye
Sing you goodbye
Sing you goodbye

1,093.

Pixies with nylon wings
And plastic wands
Blue nail polish
Striped stockings
And ruby slippers
Synchronization
Of punk rock and fairy tales
Drinking candy liquor
Carmel apples
The modern fey

1,097.

Don't leave me trapped in neverland
Stranded above the city lights
The air feels different here
Marble walls may block the view
But they don't make the real world stop
there isn't a foot of earth left
Not covered by a satellite
The television will get me
There's no place left to hide
Everyone looks so beautiful
Pity their insides don't match
You'd think they never age
But even if they don't die they rot
This isn't how the world works
The world isn't big enough
So if you can't hide in space
You have to hide in time
I chose the twenties
Though I almost picked the fifties
Dress in drop-waist skirts
Bob my hair and watch silent movies
My phonograph playing
It's a wonderful playtime
But like everything here it's not real
Just something to stave off the madness
Don't leave me here in neverland

1,091.

Anyone who would listen
Listen
Anyone who would care
Care
'Cause there's not enough listen
And not near enough care
But some is more than none
You can only improve things by adding
So if someone thinks it doesn't matter
It does

276.

I love you
That's all I have to say
That's all anyone has
That's worth saying